Original title:
The Seedling Saga

Copyright © 2025 Creative Arts Management OÜ
All rights reserved.

Author: Adrian Caldwell
ISBN HARDBACK: 978-1-80566-607-3
ISBN PAPERBACK: 978-1-80566-892-3

Colors of Hope

In a garden where laughter grows,
Tiny sprouts play peek-a-boo,
With polka-dot leaves and wild poses,
They wear sunshine like a tutu.

Dandelions dance in the breeze,
Telling jokes to the bees nearby,
"Why did the flower cross the street?"
"To get to the blooming high!"

A sunflower flexes, tall and proud,
Flashing petals at the noisy crowd,
"I'm the star of this garden show!"
While tulips giggle, putting on a bow.

They paint the soil with giggles bright,
In a world where all feels just right,
For every sprout in this playful land,
Joyful chaos at nature's hand.

The Unfolding Journey

Little seeds embark with a grin,
"Adventure awaits, let's begin!"
With a sprinkle of rain and a splash of sun,
The race to grow is oh-so-fun!

A tiny radish rolls on its side,
"Home is where the dirt is wide!"
While carrots giggle, hiding so deep,
In their cozy beds, they dream and sleep.

"Hey, Mr. Bean, how's the view?"
"Better than yours, but I'll trade with you!"
Across the plot, with roots that twist,
They barter laughter in a comedic mist.

With every inch they stretch and climb,
They make the most of their sunny time,
For it's not just about the height they gain,
But the friends they make—and the laughs they train.

Embracing the Light

Beneath the sun, with a cheeky glow,
Seedlings shout, "Look at us grow!"
With arms wide open to the bright blue sky,
They joke around, "We're not shy!"

A cactus grumbles, "Why is it hot?
I'm armed with needles, but I'm getting shot!"
While daisies bloom, play tag with the breeze,
"Join our game, if you please!"

As shadows dance, they sway and bend,
In this wild patch, all animosities end,
They sing to the moon, a tune so light,
"We're all just here to embrace the night!"

Each leaf a smile, each petal a cheer,
In the garden of giggles, there's nothing to fear,
So plant those dreams in soils divine,
And let the good times intertwine!

The Courage of the First Leaf

In a world of giants, I sprout up high,
With a wink to the sun, I reach for the sky.
A snail shouts, "Look! It's a brave little sprig!"
I chuckle and stretch, feeling so big!

Wiggly worms whisper, "You'll never make it!"
But I dance with the breeze, saying, "Just wait!"
The ants throw a party, they cheer and they cheer,
For the first little leaf who has conquered her fear!

Beneath the Canopy of Tomorrow

Under a roof of leaves, oh what a sight,
Little critters tango, all day and all night.
A squirrel named Max cracks a nut just for fun,
While I giggle and sway in the warmth of the sun.

The breeze makes me giggle, oh what a tease!
I pretend I'm a dancer, I sway with such ease.
The birds sing in harmony, a raucous delight,
Together we brighten this whimsical night.

Cradled by the Sun's Caress

The sun tickles leaves like a playful friend,
While I bask in its glow, this moment won't end.
Ladybugs bounce, they're gathering near,
"Come share in the warmth!" I call out with cheer.

A shadow might pass, oh dear, what a fright!
A bumblebee hums, "It's just me, what a sight!"
With laughter I roll, in my patch of green bliss,
I toss back a leaf, saying, "Can you top this?"

Passage of the Persistent Seed

Through mud and mishap, I made my way here,
Dodging raindrops and worms, oh never fear.
At last, I unfurl, my journey's begun,
And I wave to the clouds, saying, "Look, it's fun!"

Each day's an adventure, a chuckle, a thrill,
With every small breeze, I'm filled with goodwill.
So here I will stand, bright green and so spry,
In the grand game of growth, I'll surely fly high!

The Awakening of Nature's Soul

In the garden, sprouts arise,
Curious whispers fill the skies.
Tiny leaves start to dance and sway,
As the sun claims the brand new day.

Worms are wiggling in delight,
Poking heads out, oh what a sight!
Petals giggle as they bloom,
Nature's humor fills the room.

Dew drops sparkle, giggles squeak,
Nature's voice is far from meek.
As bees take turns in their parade,
Carrying pollen, lemonade!

So let the mischief now unfold,
With every sprout, a tale is told.
In this cacophony of cheer,
Nature's laughter, loud and clear!

Heralds of New Beginnings

Little buds on branches peek,
Sneaking out just to take a peek.
Spring is here, the air is bright,
Everything's ready for a kite flight!

The squirrels are busy, gathering snacks,
While ants march on in perfect packs.
A flower's hat tilts with a grin,
As frogs croak songs that never thin.

Raindrops dribble like giggling kids,
Splashing puddles, where fun begins.
Even the rocks join in the play,
Who knew the earth could dance this way?

So raise a toast with tiny cups,
To all the plants that won't give up.
Life's a comedy, so grand, so neat,
In nature's theater, can't be beat!

Legacy of the Endless Sky

Clouds drift by with cotton candy,
Painting shades so warm and dandy.
Sunbeams dive in silly loops,
Tickling the sides of sunny troops.

A breeze sneaks in with a hearty laugh,
Telling tales on the forest path.
Grass blades chatter, "What a day!"
"Catch the clouds! Let's have a play!"

Pollen flutters, waving cheer,
Inviting all the bees near here.
The trees sway side to side with glee,
Making music, just like a spree.

So let the sky be our big stage,
Where every joy can have its page.
With roots in fun and leaves aflutter,
Nature's legacy isn't a mutter!

The Quiet Resilience of Tender Shoots

Tiny stems push through the ground,
Whispers of strength are all around.
Each little sprout a story speaks,
Of brave adventures, silly peaks.

Nighttime giggles in the dark,
Stars twinkle down, spark by spark.
Dreams of growing tall and wide,
Behind each leaf, hopes abide.

The wind shares secrets with the buds,
As they stretch up from their cozy muds.
Even with storms, they stand so brave,
The quiet strength that they gave.

So let's cheer for the tiny greens,
For in their hearts, the world convenes.
In every sprout, a tale retold,
Of resilience, laughter, and bold gold!

Unseen Strengths

In the soil, secrets hide,
Tiny sprouts with dreams inside.
They wiggle, dance beneath the ground,
A secret strength, yet to be found.

With every rain, they stretch and yawn,
Singing tunes to greet the dawn.
Who knew such mischief lurked below?
Plotting a takeover, they steal the show!

Roots entwine like friends at play,
Whispering jokes, come what may.
While we think they simply grow,
They're planning parties—who would know?

So next time when you see them sprout,
Remember what their fun's about.
For in this world, oh what a scene,
Even plants dream big, to be seen!

The Language of the Roots

Underfoot, they chit-chat all day,
Sharing secrets in leafy ballet.
With a wink and a wiggle so sly,
Roots gossip like friends passing by.

One whispers, 'Did you hear the news?'
Another chuckles, 'I've got the blues.'
They've planned a meeting, oh what a sight,
To decide whose turn is it to take flight.

With grips and nudges, they make their case,
Fighting for sunlight, the ultimate race.
While we might think they're quiet and meek,
They're cheeky and bold—oh, what a sneak!

So as they stretch to the sky so bright,
Remember their chatter, hidden from sight.
For in the earth, where bickering blooms,
The roots have all the best inside jokes and tunes!

A Symphony of Growth

In the garden, a tune begins,
With tiny leaves, soft like skins.
The breeze hits the buds, they sway with might,
Creating music, oh what a delight!

A daisy sings in a high-pitched voice,
While the weeds below make a raucous choice.
Together they form a jolly refrain,
In this orchestra of sunshine and rain.

Every sprout, a note in the song,
Even the thorns try to play along.
Though some may grumble and try to pout,
The rhythm of nature is never in doubt!

So prance through the rows, give them some cheer,
For this green symphony is magic, my dear.
With roots in the soil and heads in the air,
Nature's ensemble is beyond compare!

The Hope Within the Soil

Beneath the weight of dirt and grime,
Hope lies hidden, waiting for time.
With a giggle and a wiggly twist,
Little dreams emerge, too good to miss.

Tickled by rain, they rise with glee,
'What adventures await us? Let's see!'
As worms take notes, the bugs applaud,
In this underground world, there's plenty to laud.

Each sprig holds wishes of joy untold,
Like tiny treasures, fearless and bold.
They break through the earth, full of surprise,
With a wink and a leap, they aim for the skies!

So plant a smile in your heart each day,
For in the soil, hopes find their way.
With laughter and light, just like they show,
The magic of growth is a wondrous flow!

Burgeoning Wonders of the Wild

In the garden, a sprout had a fray,
Trying to dance in a light, breezy sway.
It twisted and turned, gave a clumsy twirl,
Calling the bugs for an impromptu whirl.

The veggies all giggled, the herbs rolled their eyes,
As the sprout lost its balance, oh what a surprise!
It landed on onions with a comical thud,
And declared it was nothing but a green, gooey mud!

The Promise of a New Horizon

A bean sprout claimed it could reach the sky,
With dreams of a throne, oh my, oh my!
It stretched its leaves high, proud as can be,
While peas told it, 'Dude, just wait and see!'

The clouds gathered round, bursting with laughter,
As the sprout shouted back, 'I'm a green, leafy master!'
But just like a kid on a swing gone too far,
It fell back to earth, now a budding superstar!

Beneath the Surface

Down in the dirt where the worms like to play,
Roots whispered secrets all night and day.
They giggled of dreams, the veggies took flight,
While potatoes discussed their plans for the night.

A carrot yelled, 'Listen! I've got a big goal,
To grow really long and to steal all the soul!'
But radishes snickered, 'Oh, please, not again!
Just try not to trip on your roots, little friend!'

Life Thrives

In the sunlight, the lettuce had flair,
With leaves all a-twirl, it danced on the air.
The tomatoes chimed in, they were quite a sight,
With smiles so big, they lit up the night.

But then came the bunny, all quick and quite sly,
Looking for snacks, oh my, oh my!
The veggies all shouted, 'Ain't this a twist!
We thought we were thriving, not on a bunny's list!'

A Chronicle of Green Aspirations

There once was a sprout with a heart full of dreams,
Of climbing tall trees and starlight gleams.
It practiced its skills, leaping up high,
With a gopher below, shouting, 'Oh give it a try!'

The daisies all giggled, 'Your dreams are so big!'
But the sprout just smiled, 'Watch out, I'm a twig!'
And with a final bounce, it soared through the air,
Landed on a cabbage, with pom-poms to share!

Murmurs of the Verdant Realm

In a garden of giggles, sprouts began to play,
Each leaf a little joker, brightening the day.
A carrot wore a top hat, quite elegantly,
While tomatoes danced a jig, so cheerfully.

The radishes were pranksters, hiding out of sight,
Sneaking peeks at sunflowers, feeling quite uptight.
With whispers of laughter, the veggies took a stance,
In this leafy kingdom, they were ready to dance.

Dawn of a Thousand Greens

At dawn, the greens stretch, yawning wide and free,
A kale's a little grumpy, can't you see?
Spinach twirls in circles, a real leafy feat,
While peas pop like popcorn, a playful treat.

Celery's a comedian, with crunches so loud,
Telling all the other veggies, 'I'm really proud!'
The sun beams down warmly, like laughter on a breeze,
In this bright, funny realm, the plants aim to please.

Life's Unseen Pathways

Roots are plotting journeys in the soil below,
Searching for the sunlight, like stars in a show.
A dandelion whispers, 'Let's soar up so high!'
While grasshoppers laugh, leaping into the sky.

Along unseen pathways where the critters roam,
Mice throw a wild party, it's a veggie home!
The thrill of the chase, what a wacky pull,
As plants join the fun, their hearts are never dull.

From Humble Beginnings to Great Heights

Once a tiny seed, so small and quite shy,
Dreaming of the world, where the butterflies fly.
Now a proud sunflower, with a grin oh so wide,
Chasing after rainbows, growing with pride.

A sprout's clumsy and wobbly, stumbles a bit,
But with twists and turns, it never will quit.
In this quirky playground, where the earthworms dig,
The journey's a riot, each day's a new gig.

Roots in the Whispering Wind

In the garden so bright, where the daisies twirl,
A dance of the roots with a giggle and whirl.
The carrots conspire with the sweet little peas,
Telling tall tales as they sway in the breeze.

With rhubarb and radish plotting a prank,
They tie up the lettuce, who gives a loud clank.
The chives have a laugh, growing taller each day,
As they tickle the air in their own special way.

The onions all weep at the stories they hear,
While the cabbage just rolls and mutters, "Oh dear!"
The broccoli chuckles, all green and so proud,
"Let's all burst out laughing; let's cheer loud and loud!"

And when the sun sets, the giggles won't cease,
As the buds share their secrets, their laughter is peace.

Nature's Gentle Awakening

When springtime arrives, with daffodils spry,
The tulips stand tall, with their heads held up high.
They tickle the bees, dancing carefree in flight,
While the daisies debate if it's warmer at night.

A bunny hops in, with large floppy ears,
Who jokes with the flowers, it's good for their cheers.
The sunflowers grin, as they reach for the sky,
Translation of sunlight, with giggles nearby.

The ladybugs gather to play hide and seek,
Wagering on petals, all rosy and meek.
The earthworms are laughing, all wriggly in ground,
"O what fun we have when spring comes around!"

So join in the fun when Nature's awake,
With all her creations, each giggle they make.

Stories of Starlit Sprouts

Underneath the moon, where the tiny seeds play,
They whisper their dreams in the soft light of day.
One wants to grow tall like the tallest of pines,
While another declares to win best of the vines.

With a wink of a leaf, the oak shares a tale,
Of storms that they've faced, and how they prevail.
The dandelions giggle, their fluff blowing free,
As they plot little mischief with glee by the tree.

"Let's fly far and wide!" the small sprouts all cry,
"On the backs of the winds, we will wave goodbye."
They twirl and they twist, telling jokes from the past,
"Remember the crow? Oh, he was such a blast!"

And as dawn approaches, their laughter takes flight,
For stories of stars will keep shining so bright.

From Darkness, Life Emerges

Deep in the soil, where it's dark and it's damp,
Little seeds gather round, like a sleepy old camp.
They whisper of sunlight, both golden and warm,
And the joys of the rain that helps them transform.

Each one has a story, a dream of the sky,
"I'll grow up to be tall!" one will puff and will sigh.
"No, I'll twist and turn, and I'll creep on the ground,"
They chuckle and wiggle with laughter abound.

The mushrooms are here, with their caps looking grand,
They pop up to join in the sprout's friendly band.
"We'll have a great party when growth starts to soar,
With roots that do tango, who could ask for more?"

From darkness they rise, with a giggle and cheer,
In a world full of light, they have nothing to fear.

Whispers of New Growth

A tiny sprout with a lot to say,
Wiggling its leaves in a bright ballet.
"Don't step on me, I'm not a rug!"
It giggles softly, feeling snug.

The sun peeks down with a warm, big grin,
"Grow up big, like a leafy kin!"
But watch out for crows with their beady eyes,
They think we're salad, oh what a surprise!

When raindrops come, they dance and play,
"Here comes a shower, let's surf today!"
They splash and splatter in a merry group,
Nature's party, oh what a scoop!

As time goes on, they'll sprout and bloom,
Each little plant with its own costume.
A carnival of colors, a laugh-filled spree,
In the garden stage, where all are free!

Beneath the Earth's Embrace

Down in the dirt, there's a ruckus of cheer,
The worms are singing, and they're not even here!
"We're on a quest, to make you fat,"
They wiggle with glee, wearing a big hat.

The seedlings shout from their cozy bed,
"What's cooking down there? We're all so fed!"
The mycelium shares a joke or two,
"Try my mushroom soup, it's a fungi stew!"

With roots entwined like a tangled dance,
They plot sweet mischief, a daring chance.
"Let's send the humans on a wild goose chase,
While we conquer the world at our own pace!"

Oh, the laughter echoes in nature's tight place,
Where friendships blossom with a touch of grace.
Beneath the earth, tales twist and curl,
In the hidden realm, it's a fun-filled whirl!

A Journey from Soil to Sky

With a nudge and a push, out pops a head,
From cozy soil, where it once was fed.
"Whoa, what is this? I'm not alone!"
The sprout looks around, feeling overthrown.

"Hey, look at me! I'm taller than you!"
A cheeky little sprig said with a view.
"Let's reach for the clouds and touch the sun,"
They giggle and stretch, that's how it's done!

A breeze tickles gently, they wave with flair,
"Beware, dear birds, our leaves are rare!"
The flowers are blooming, it's a colorful sight,
With every new bud, oh what delight!

Each one's a story, a sketch to unfold,
Of brave little seedlings, both timid and bold.
From soil to the sky, they dance and sway,
In the light of the sun, they play all day!

Budding Dreams and Tiny Tales

In a land of green, where dreams are spun,
Tiny tales whisper, oh what fun!
"Once I was a nut, now I'm a tree!"
Laughs a little acorn, proud as can be.

The daisies gossip under the sun,
"Do you hear that? It's the scuffle of fun!"
As the ants march by with food to share,
"Hey, want a snack? It's a fancy affair!"

The clouds drift lazily, deciding who's best,
"I'm fluffier than you!" they proudly jest.
While the sun plays peek-a-boo with the blooms,
Tickling their petals, dispelling the glooms.

In this magical realm, every sprout's a star,
With dreams in their hearts, they reach near and far.
Budding stories await in the garden's embrace,
Where laughter and joy always finds a place!

The Embrace of Rain and Sun

A droplet smiled on a leafy face,
The sun winked down, a warm embrace.
They danced together, a quirky pair,
Splashing clouds with laughter in the air.

The bugs joined in with a buzzing cheer,
As raindrops played, the sky would leer.
With mud on their shoes, they splashed and spun,
This silly game had just begun!

A flower blushed beneath the spout,
"Hey, don't soak me!" it did shout out.
The sun just giggled, "I'll dry you fast!"
And so their friendship was made to last.

Underneath the arch of rainbow bright,
Nature's spectacle a pure delight.
With rain and sun, what fun awaits—
A party blooms from nature's gates!

Tales Written in Nature's Ink

A dandelion puffed, feeling grand,
Wrote secret tales in the soft, warm sand.
The winds would giggle at the stories spread,
As squirrels sat down, all ears and dread.

"Once upon a leaf," said the tall green grass,
"Bravest of buds, who wanted to pass!"
With whispers of bees and chirps from the tree,
The plot thickened, oh, what would it be?

"Then came a storm!" a brook said with glee,
"Who tossed the old branches, quite carefree!"
But laughter erupted from an old rusty gate,
"I'm more of a saga; let's not hesitate!"

Under the sky, they shared and they melded,
Nature spins yarns and most never held it.
With giggles and gaffes etched in wind's ink,
Life's delightful dance makes everyone think!

Flourishing in the Face of Adversity

A sprout peeked out through the stubborn soil,
   Said, "I'm not afraid! I'll toil and toil!"
With tiny roots that wiggled and squirmed,
   It shouted to rocks, "You'll be outperformed!"

The clouds grumbled, "Rain may not come,"
But the sprout just chuckled, "Oh, I'll be fun!"
"Bring on the drought, or fierce winds of fate,
   I'll dance like a leaf, no room for hate!"

"Who needs sunshine?" it shouted with glee,
"I thrive in shadows where no one can see!"
With bravado and grit, it basked in the gloom,
   An unexpected flower dared to bloom!

Oh, adversity laughed, what a jester it was,
   Stirring the pot with a cheeky buzz.
But laughter erupted, as roots all entwined,
   In the face of it all, true grit you will find!

The Chronicles of Bursting Buds

A bud stretched wide, a bit too keen,
"I'll beat the others; they're hardly seen!"
It puffed out proud, with petals prepped,
But tripped on a vine, oh, the laughter wept!

"Watch me explode!" it hollered so bright,
But only a sigh, what a pitiful sight.
While nearby a weed took the lead with flair,
"Hey, I'm no flower, but I don't care!"

A crush of colors in a hilarious fight,
All vying for glory, oh, what a sight!
Petals and leaves covered in mud,
They laughed at the chaos of nature's flood.

In the end, each bloom found a place,
Despite silly stumbles, each had their grace.
With chuckles and winks, the garden would sing,
For in the mishaps, a funny joy springs!

The Budding Adventurer

There once was a sprout, so brave and bold,
It dreamt of adventures, tales yet untold.
It aimed for the sky, with a wink and a twist,
Said, "I'll be famous, just wait till I'm kissed!"

The ants laughed and danced, all dressed in their best,
"A sprout on a quest? Now that's quite the jest!"
But off it did go, a tiny green knight,
With a leaf for a shield and a stem ever bright!

A butterfly landed, said, "You look fun!"
The sprout puffed up proud, "Just wait—I've begun!"
With roots in the soil and sun overhead,
It plotted to conquer, a world still unread!

So if you see sprouts with big dreams and plans,
Remember their journeys, the great little fans.
For even the smallest can wish and explore,
Who knows what they'll do when they open their door!

Nature's Gentle Revolution

Beneath the thick soil, a whisper made way,
A chorus of seedlings decided, "Let's play!"
"We'll turn over rocks, we'll stand up and shout,"
"It's time for a change, let's not be without!"

The daisies kept giggling, the lilies in line,
"All hail the brave sprouts, they think they are fine!"
But roots intertwined, they rallied anew,
"Together we'll grow, we'll shake up the dew!"

The weeds waved their flags, while clouds joined the fun,

Announcing new growth with a glittering sun.
They danced in the breeze, spread joy all around,
"Nature's so clever, who knew it was profound?"

With laughter and joy, the revolution thrived,
Each sprout with a grin, in the sunshine arrived.
And when springtime brushed over all that they knew,
The world turned to green, and the clouds burst anew!

Rising Through the Cracks

A brave little plant pushed through the hard stone,
"Hello, world!" it sang, in a voice all its own.
With grit in its roots and a stretch in its leaf,
It giggled, "Hah! I'm beyond belief!"

A sidewalk observer, a squirrel in disguise,
Chortled and chirped, "Look at that! What a surprise!"
"You think you're so tough, in this crack you've found?"
"Well, I'm a tough nut, and I'm living unbound!"

It leaned to the sun, a very proud sneak,
"I'll grow my own shade; I don't need to be sleek!"
With dandelion dreams and a wink from the sky,
The tiny plant laughed, "No limits apply!"

Through concrete and chaos, it thrived with a cheer,
"For every cracked sidewalk, a flower will appear!"
So here's to the plants who break through with grace,
In the oddest of places, they find their own space!

A Tale of Leaves and Shadows

In the forest so bright, where the leaves play their games,
Lived whimsical shadows, each with funny names.
"Here comes Wobbly Willow, and Flippy McLeaf!"
"Don't forget Sneaky Shade, the master of mischief!"

They'd hide from the sun, giggling under trees,
Tickling the branches in a playful breeze.
"Come join our parade! We'll dance on the grass!"
Chanted the leaves as the critters ran past.

With acorns a'clatter and pinecones all round,
The shadows did spin, laughing, never to drown.
"Let's paint the wind blue, and the sun's rays all pink!"
"Let's prank those tall trees! What do you think?"

So they twirled through the woods, with glee in each step,

Creating wild stories no one could forget.
For in laughter and shade, the leaves found their song,
And ever since then, shadows danced all day long!

Secrets Carried on a Breeze

A tiny seed with dreams so grand,
Told the wind, "Take me to a land!"
With whispers soft and winks so sly,
It danced away, oh my, oh my!

The breeze just giggled, oh what a tease,
"You're just a sprout, oh please, oh please!"
With every gust, a chuckle flew,
"Let's see what nonsense you can do!"

Through fields it floated, swelling pride,
A saga spun, as it did glide.
"Just wait and watch, I'll grow so tall!
I'll shade your path! I'll be the wall!"

But when it landed, oh what a sight,
A patch of weeds—it took a bite!
The seed had hoped for lands so bright,
Yet feasted on weeds, its dream in flight!

Stories Told by Tiny Tendrils

Once a sprout with stories vast,
Whispered its tale from root to fast!
"Oh, listen close, to what I say,
I'll grow so strong, just watch today!"

Its tendrils twisted, curled, and swirled,
Searching for secrets in the world.
With every poke, they tickled grass,
Telling tales that made others laugh!

"I'll cling to fences, swing from trees,
Just watch me dance in the warm breeze!"
But all the plants just rolled their eyes,
"You're just a sprout with silly lies!"

Yet still it laughed and spun around,
For every giggle was magic found.
It knew one day, it'd reach the sun,
A leafy champ, the wisest one!

An Odyssey of Green

A little bean set sail one day,
Across the garden, it did play!
Climbing on dreams and dirt so deep,
It plotted tales while others sleep.

"An odyssey for me," it grinned,
With tiny leaves that swayed and sinned!
Each raindrop whispered "Grow, be bold!"
"For adventure waits in tales of old!"

Through mud and muck, it found its way,
Past grumpy rocks that had much to say.
"Watch out, you sprout! Don't trip or flop!"
With every laugh, it wouldn't stop.

And when it bloomed, oh what a cheer!
It waved at bugs, "Come gather here!"
A journey spun, a garden tale,
Of beans and dreams that would not fail!

Bursting Forth into the Light

A timid sprout stretched out a leaf,
"Am I too small?" it asked in grief.
Then sunlight chuckled, warm and bright,
"Get ready, friend, with all your might!"

With every wiggle and twist it made,
It blasted up, not just a shade!
"Ready or not, here I come!" it cried,
As flowers waved and roots supplied.

The world below was filled with dirt,
While up above, it wore a shirt!
Of vibrant greens, it danced around,
"Who knew that joy could be this sound?"

With blossoms bright and pollen sweet,
It threw a party for each leaf meet.
A jubilee of fun and flight,
As every grower burst forth into the light!

The Dance of Green Aspirations

In a garden where giggles sprout,
Little greens leap about,
With roots that twist and turn,
Doing the dance they yearn.

Tiny sprouts in a jolly parade,
Wiggling bodies, they're unafraid,
They twirl and spin in the sun's bright hue,
Bouncing around like they're in a zoo.

Seedlings in hats made of blooms,
Twisting on their leafy plumes,
With the bees joining their jive,
Making sure the garden's alive.

Together they laugh, such a warm sight,
Underneath the moon's soft light,
Sending vibes that make you grin,
Oh, the joy beneath the skin!

Echoes of the Sprouting Heart

In a patch where laughter grows,
Tiny seeds share their woes,
Complaining of worms in their beds,
While dreaming of castles in their heads.

The petals with a giggle sway,
Chasing the clouds that drift away,
They whisper tales of the sun's warm glow,
As they plan to outshine the row.

Roots deep down in silly chats,
Critiquing the antics of passing cats,
Reveling in the dirt's cool embrace,
With dreams of a big leafy space.

As sunlight slips in for a peek,
The greens rehearse a comedic streak,
A sprouting heart beats bold and bright,
Giggling beneath the starry night!

Threads of Hope in Dappled Light

In the weave of sunlit beams,
Little shoots share their dreams,
With shadows playing hide and seek,
In a world where joy is sleek.

The leaves whisper in harmony,
Threads of hope like a symphony,
Each petal waving an eager hand,
Sailing on laughter like a band.

Dancing on winds that softly blow,
Sowing cheer as they grow,
Each stem with tales of ticklish glee,
Sharing secrets of what could be.

As dusk wraps its arms around,
The night brings a crinkly sound,
With giggling roots beneath the surface,
Creating joy, that's their true purpose!

Unfurling Secrets of the Ground

Beneath the earth, where whispers dwell,
Secrets of nature weave a spell,
Tales of mischief from below,
Of daisies learning how to flow.

Each sprout tells a quirky tale,
Of jumping over a tiny snail,
With dreams of colors, bold and bright,
And giggles echoing through the night.

Unfurling arms stretching wide,
Hoping for a fun-filled ride,
They wiggle and dance as they emerge,
In a choir of joy, they surge.

Under stars that twinkle and wink,
The little ones find time to think,
With every laugh, the soil finds grace,
In this funny, green-filled place!

The Language of Leaves and Breezes

In the garden, leaves do chatter,
Whispers shared, as they all splatter.
Breezes giggle with a soft sway,
Dancing lightly, come what may.

Laughter grows from roots to tips,
Even worms join in with flips.
Petals cup their tiny tea,
Sharing jokes just between the tree.

A ladybug in her bright red shell,
Claims the throne, a bug queen's spell.
While ants march with synchronized strife,
Thinking they're leading the good life.

Together, they spin stories anew,
Beneath a sky so very blue.
For in this patch of sunlit ground,
Funny secrets are all around.

Dreams Planted in Deep Earth

Seeds hatch dreams beneath the soil,
Tangled roots in a merry coil.
Worms wear chef hats, cooking up fun,
Prepping plots for everyone.

Popping up like a sproutled clown,
Dancing up, never feeling down.
Sunbeams tickle tiny green heads,
A laughter chorus among the beds.

Squirrels plan their acorn heist,
While shooting stars drop crumbs on insist.
In the dark of night, they might scheme,
But it's all in the garden's dream.

Every pebble hums a new tune,
As daisies sway beneath the moon.
From deep earth to the wide, bright sky,
The playful dance will always fly.

The Struggles of the Small

In the dirt, the tiny fight,
A sprout struggles with all its might.
Pushing through the earthy embrace,
Facing the odds with a determined face.

Every raindrop feels like a burst,
But they march on, quenching their thirst.
With each wobble, they're learning grace,
In this grand, green, fabulous race.

Ants march past, they laugh and brag,
"What's a sprout next to our flag?"
Yet the tiny green stands ever tall,
Soon they'll shine, the bravest of all.

Roots tangle in their own silly way,
Plotting promise for a brighter day.
For every struggle is a tale to tell,
In the saga where small things dwell.

Triumph of the Tender Green

Sheep clouds fluff the bright blue sky,
While tender greens confidently sigh.
A patch of carrots wears glasses, too,
Reading stories of what they knew.

Grasshoppers compete in a leap-frog race,
Cheering loudly in a leafy space.
The sun-splashed roots hold hands and cheer,
As the triumph of green draws near.

Pansies giggle at the sassy breeze,
Entwined in laughter between the trees.
For every shadow hints at a joke,
In the chatter where fresh dreams provoke.

With colors bright, they light the scene,
The garden thrives, so joyous and keen.
In this whimsical world, they'll reign,
The tender green will never wane.

Petals in the Dawn's Embrace

In the morning light they dance,
Little sprouts with a chance.
Wiggly roots tickle the ground,
What silly sights can be found!

The daisies wear their best frowns,
While tulips giggle in gowns.
Bumblebees buzz like they're late,
Flowers prank, it's all first-rate!

Morning dew like a sweet treat,
Grass blades quiver, they can't beat.
The sun peeks in, oh what a sight,
Petals wink, oh what delight!

With a sigh, the flowers sway,
"Another funny, silly day!"
As blooms stretch out to greet,
Nature's joys are oh so sweet!

The Legacy of Renewal

In a garden full of cheer,
Old plants whisper, "We're still here!"
A sprout jumps up with a grin,
"Watch me twirl, let's begin!"

Earthworms sing their squirmy song,
Dancing to the roots all day long.
As new buds peek and shout,
"Hey, old pals, what's this about?"

Leaves high-five in a leafy spree,
While gnomes giggle, "Can't you see?"
The cycle keeps rolling on,
In goofy glee from dusk till dawn.

Raising a toast with soil cups,
To all the buttercup hiccups!
Renewal brings laughter and play,
In this silly, leafy ballet!

Journey of the Tender Sprout

A tiny seed with dreams to grow,
Poked its head up, "Hello, Whoa!"
Wiggling through the soil with flair,
"I'm sprouting here, just take a chair!"

The big oak laughed, "Not so fast!
Your journey's long, don't tire, don't blast!"
But the sprout bounced, "I've got hope,
I'll stretch my leaves and learn to cope!"

One day a breeze gave a shove,
"Don't sway too much, you've got to love!"
The sprout twirled in the sun's soft glow,
"I won't stop! Just watch me go!"

With each raindrop, the fun unfolds,
Adventure awaits in tales untold.
Sprouting high, taking a bow,
A tiny hero, look at me now!

Echoes of the Bursting Buds

In a bloom-filled choir they sing,
Budlets bursting, what joy they bring!
Chirping crickets playing along,
Nature's laughter is their song.

Dandelions shout, "What's our perk?"
As sunflowers join with a smirk.
"Who knew we'd be such a hit?
Let's put on a show, let's make it lit!"

With petals stretched out wide and bright,
Bursting buds steal the spotlight.
Echoes of giggles float on air,
Plants sharing secrets everywhere.

Beneath the moon, they sway and cheer,
Each little bud holds joy so near.
The dance of life, so full of glee,
In a garden where everyone's free!

Breath of the Earth

In the soil where whispers dwell,
Little roots cast quite a spell.
Wiggling worms start their dance,
Planting dreams of leafy romance.

Raindrops fall like giggling rains,
Tickling leaves with their playful strains.
The sun winks down, a golden grin,
As buds blush softly, where laughs begin.

The Silent Surge

Beneath the ground, a secret game,
A sprout's ambition to make a name.
With tiny fists, it pushes up,
Imagining itself as a mighty cup.

The daisies cheer with petals wide,
While ants march on, strutting with pride.
A snail joins in, unsure of the score,
Yet slides along, hungry for more.

From Seed to Symphony

A seed once small, now a tall tale,
Bouncing around like a wind-blown sail.
Chirping birds join the ensemble,
While squirrels dance, oh so nimble!

Sunshine beats a rhythmic thrum,
While bees hum along, creating a drum.
The breeze provides a soft serenade,
As nature laughs at the grand parade.

Resilience in Green

A leaf fell down from the tallest tree,
Said, 'Hey, look at me, I'm wild and free!'
Others nodded, full of glee,
'Let's roll around, just you and me!'

The branches swayed, a funky twist,
Though windy days might be hard to resist.
But laughter echoes through the glade,
In this green valley, joy's not delayed.

Threads of Roots and Dreams

In the soil, a tiny dream,
Laughter bubbles, bursting seam.
With a wiggle, it sways,
Sipping rain on sunny days.

Roots were tangled, quite a mess,
Worms were dancing in their dress.
'This way up!' cried the little sprout,
'No, down! We're all lost, there's no doubt!'

Bumbles bees, in silly flight,
Buzzed along, joining the plight.
Pulling at strings, what a show,
'The more we pull, the more we grow!'

Petals giggled, leaves would cheer,
Behind the clouds, the sun drew near.
With a twirl, they bloomed in style,
"We're a garden—what a smile!"

The Awakening Sprouts

Waking up, the little buds,
Poking heads from out of floods.
"Look at us, we're quite a sight!"
"Hey, who turned on the sunlight?"

The garden gnome, with his old hat,
Tried to catch the chirping chat.
"Mind if I join this morning spree?"
"Sure, but don't spill your tea!"

With the breeze, a tickling tick,
Tiny leaves begin to flick.
"I'm a dancer!" one declared,
While another twirled, unscared.

Seeds did giggle, roots did roast,
"Who knew we'd turn into this host?"
Smiles all around, a joyful throng,
In a world where sproutlings belong.

Journey of the Tender Shoot

A journey starts with tiny steps,
Through puddles with strange insect rep's.
"Look, a snail! How slow can he be?"
"Faster than us, but that's just me!"

Up above, the bluebirds sing,
While beneath, earthworms do their thing.
"Ouch! Watch your toes, how rude!"
"Sorry, but I'm just a sprouting dude!"

With every stretch, they looked around,
"What a world—so big, profound!"
A dandelion waved hello,
While ants marched in a perfect row.

"I hope they don't bring us back," said one,
As the sun shone down, day begun.
"We'll be giants, just you wait,
With our laughter, it'll be great!"

Echoes of Nature's Promise

The whispers of leaves, secrets unfold,
Stories of growth that never get old.
"Why'd you grow sideways?" one plant asked,
"Just exploring, is that so unmasked?"

On a breeze, sweet scents collide,
While grumpy roots grumble, "Take pride!"
"Why not dance, twist, and twirl?"
"Only if you share that whirl!"

Breezes chuckle, carrying song,
Melodies simple, where sprouts belong.
"Dance with us, don't be shy!"
"Alright, but only if we try!"

Together they played, a lively scene,
Cheerful chaos, fittingly green.
Finding joy in the goof and glee,
In the garden, so wild and free.

Harmony in a Garden of Dreams

In the garden where giggles bloom,
A carrot whispers, "Make some room!"
The radishes dance in bright, fierce hues,
While tomatoes wear the silliest shoes.

The butterflies chuckle, flapping their wings,
As beetles conduct, leading the swings.
"I'm the queen of this colorful mess!"
Said a bold sunflower, adorned in excess.

A rainbow of veggies, with tales to tell,
Swap stories of growing in the soft swell.
"Hey, lettuce!" shouts a cheeky green bean,
"Let's plan a party, to keep this scene!"

With laughter aplenty, they plot and scheme,
In the heart of the garden, every leaf gleams.
Joy sprouts like daisies, so wild and free,
In this patchwork of whims, oh what glee!

The Awakening of Forgotten Fields

In fields once sleepy, now lively and bright,
The old scarecrow chuckles at the new light.
"Why the long faces? Come dance with me!"
Said a peppy little flower, as sweet as can be.

A tumbleweed waltzes, spins with flair,
While daisies gossip and giggle with care.
"Remember when we were just seeds in the dirt?"
Laughed a proud onion, still wearing its shirt.

The corn starts to boogie, with is a loud pop,
While pumpkins roll over, refusing to stop.
"Let's raise a ruckus!" the roots all declare,
"We'll throw a fiesta! Now, who'll bring the fare?"

With petals and laughter, the night comes alive,
In the fields of dreams, where the jests thrive.
Who knew that a patch could harbor such fun,
In the dance of the crops, we're all number one!

A Symphony of Rising Shoots

From the soil emerged a bold little sprout,
"Who said I couldn't grow tall? Let's shout!"
As leaves played the trumpets, roots played the drums,
The garden erupted, oh how it hums!

A daffodil solo, sweet notes in the air,
As carrots joined in, full of flair!
"Who hit the high notes? It must be the pea!"
Laughed the broccoli, swaying with glee.

Their laughter was music, a delightful tune,
While clouds joined the party, round like a moon.
"Oh look, here comes the rain, what a show!"
Hollered a radish, ready to glow.

In this orchestra of green, all played their part,
With giggles and roots, they danced from the heart.
A symphony! Oh, how the garden sings,
Of shoots and their joy, and the joy that spring brings!

Tales Written in Earth and Rain

In mud so rich, tales come alive,
Where worms weave stories that jive.
"Did you hear? The sun once fell asleep!"
Said a cheerful mushroom, secrets to keep.

The rain drops laughed as they splashed and spun,
Painting the ground, saying, "Let's have fun!"
A beetle chimed in with a tickling jest,
"Who's got the best dance? I'll be the best dressed!"

The daisies burst out in a fierce debate,
On who had the best sun-kissed fate.
With roots entwined and hearts set aglow,
"Let's write our saga! It's time to grow!"

With laughter and love, these tales came to be,
In the heart of the garden, wild and free.
Every drop of rain held a giggle, a cheer,
In stories of earth, we all persevere!

A Dance with Sunlight

A tiny sprout in morning's glow,
Wobbles and jiggles, putting on a show.
With rays of gold, it twirls with glee,
Swaying to rhythms, just wait and see!

A worm joins in, with a wiggly twist,
They dance together, too cute to resist.
The breeze becomes music, oh what a scene,
Even the daisies flash smiles, so keen!

Sunshine chuckles at their silly prance,
But looks away - it can't take the chance!
For if it dazzles too brightly, you see,
These goofy dancers, might grow a little too free!

As shadows stretch on the garden floor,
The little sprout hums, "I want to explore!"
But bedtime comes, with a snoozy yawn,
And dreams of the dawn, as night carries on.

Hidden in the Earth's Cradle

Down below where the darkness thrums,
A world of wonders, where life hums.
A seed with a giggle, snuggled tight,
Whispers to roots, "Let's have some fun tonight!"

The beetles chat gossip, the moss likes to tease,
As critters cavort in the cool earth's ease.
"Did you hear?" said a worm with flair,
"Up top they dance, but down here it's rare!"

"Let's play hide and seek," said the sprout with a grin,
Where light can't reach, our games can begin!
A beetle peeked out, "You won't find me!"
While the roots all chuckled, "Oh, this is the key!"

Then a thought zoomed by, a thought of the sun,
"Maybe one day, this hiding is done!"
But for now, the earth's cradle they cherish,
With laughter and secrets, they'll never perish.

Flourishing in Quiet Places

In corners where shadows softly recline,
A timid green sprout dreams of sunshine.
It stretches and yawns in a bashful display,
Trying to bloom in its own quirky way!

A ladybug lands with a curious stare,
"Hey little buddy, do you ever despair?"
With a wink, it replied, "Why fret and why fuss?
I'll rise like the sun, but first, take a bus!"

In the heart of the bloom, a couple of bees,
Buzz with a laugh, "Let's throw in some cheese!"
They feasted on petals, such a fresh brew,
Laughter echoed as the sprout blushed anew.

While squirrels above held wild parties with flair,
The quiet sprout knew it mustn't compare.
It giggled and jiggled, stood tall dreams they're sewn,
For in every small nook, great adventures are grown!

Chronicles of Life's Ascent

Once a mere speck, too small to see,
Now a bold sprout, climbing up the tree.
With every inch gained, more mischief in mind,
"A leaf in the wind? I'll twist and unwind!"

The squirrels, they squeak, with a cheeky little grin,
"Has anyone told you where the fun shall begin?"
It whispered back softly, "I'm ready to soar!"
A flight of possibilities, just waiting in store!

Each raindrop a riot, each ray of delight,
A slapstick ascent to great heights from a fright.
Each struggle a giggle, each victory sweet,
With pals in the canopy, oh what a feat!

When tall tales are shared at the close of the day,
Sprouts dream of tomorrows, while squirrels shout "Hooray!"
Their journey is silly, in ways that amuse,
In the chronicles of life, it's laughter they choose!

Visions of Tomorrow in Nature's Seed

A tiny sprout in the crack of the street,
Dreams of becoming a plant that's elite.
With big leafy arms, it waves in the breeze,
Thinking of glory, while tickling the bees.

It whispers to clouds, 'Please rain on my head!'
While a snail jogs by, in a race he misread.
'I'll grow big and tall, a sight to behold!'
But for now, it just hopes to escape from the cold.

Roots wiggle underground, having fun in their play,
Counting bugs as they scurry, away from the sway.
Each blade of grass giggles, with quite the spree,
Sharing wild tales of what they could be.

In dreams of the night, it throws a grand ball,
With daisies and daisies, they dance one and all.
The moon shines above in a whimsical grin,
While the seedling just hopes it could one day fit in.

Whispers of New Beginnings

A seed on the ground says, 'What's next for me?'
'To sprout up a storm or just chill by the tree?'
The sun giggles loud, 'You'll grow with some flair!'
'Just reach for the sky, and breathe in that air!'

The ants march along in a line so straight,
While butterflies flutter, deciding their fate.
They ask the young seed if it's ready to bloom,
But it just rolls over, 'I'm enjoying this gloom!'

Concerns of the soil all add to the jest,
Saying, 'What if I'm short? Will you think I'm the best?'
Yet worms in their humor, say with a cheer,
'You're just getting started, the world isn't near!'

So the seed wiggles and shakes with glee,
Now fully convinced that it's fun just to be.
It dreams of bright flowers and veggies galore,
While the sun sets softly—oh, what's in store!

Beneath the Soil's Embrace

Down in the dirt, where the fun never ends,
The radish and carrot are best of friends.
They giggle and plot how to escape from their row,
While the potatoes just chuckle, with nowhere to go.

"My leaves are so pretty!" the cabbage will boast,
While everyone's thinking, "He's mostly just toast!"
The rhubarb rolls over, laughing as well,
Saying, "You're a decoration, it's easy to tell!"

They have late-night chats about handling pests,
While dodging the shovel like they are the best.
Sharing grand stories of rain and the sun,
And how to grow big till the day is all done.

But when morning arrives, they get quite the fright,
As above ground awaits a most curious sight.
With weeds all around, and a lawnmower too,
They hold onto dreams of what garden life could do!

Guardian of the Green

In the realm of the garden, where laughter takes root,
A brave little seedling puts on its best suit.
With petals like armor and hope in the air,
It vows to protect all who dare to be rare!

The bugs come in droves, with mischief at hand,
But the seedling stands tall, it makes its grand stand.
'You'll not munch on my friends, or cause them despair!'
As the ladybug giggles, it starts to prepare.

Chasing away fliers with arms open wide,
It befriends a wise snail who slides in with pride.
Together they plot, oh such schemes to reveal,
An anthem of green for all plants to feel!

'We're guardians of laughter, defenders of cheer!'
The sunflower nods, while the wildflowers cheer.
And as twilight falls, they settle in glee,
In a world without worries, just happy and free.

www.ingramcontent.com/pod-product-compliance
Lightning Source LLC
Chambersburg PA
CBHW071816160426
43209CB00003B/110